Charles Edwin Bennett

Syllabus of Lectures on Roman Antiquities

Charles Edwin Bennett

Syllabus of Lectures on Roman Antiquities

ISBN/EAN: 9783744773980

Printed in Europe, USA, Canada, Australia, Japan

Cover: Foto ©ninafisch / pixelio.de

More available books at **www.hansebooks.com**

SYLLABUS OF LECTURES

ON

ROMAN ANTIQUITIES

BY

CHARLES E. BENNETT
CORNELL UNIVERSITY

ITHACA
ANDRUS & CHURCH
1899

INTRODUCTION.

LECTURE I.

1. Purpose and plan of course.
2. Bibliography.
3. Sketch of Roman civilization.
   (*a*) Regal period, 753-509 B.C.—Stages :
   (1) Patriarchal state.
   (2) Priest-kings : Numa, Ancus.
   (3) Warrior kings : the Tarquins.—Indications of an Etruscan conquest.
   (4) Overthrow of the kings (expulsion of the Tarquins) and establishment of the Republic, 509 B.C.
   (*b*) The Early Republic, 509-367 B.C.—Strife of Patricians and Plebeians.
   (1) Early republic aristocratic.
   (2) Secession of the Plebeians—Institution of tribunes, 494 B.C.
   (3) Decemviral Legislation, 449 B.C.
   (4) Canuleian Law—Right of intermarriage, 445 B.C.
   (5) Licinian Rogations, 367 B.C.—Equalization of the Orders.
   (*c*) The conquest of Italy, 367-275 B.C.
   (1) Latin War, 340 B.C.
   (2) Samnite War, 295 B.C.
   (3) War with Pyrrhus, 275 B.C.
   (*d*) The conquest of the world, 275-146 B.C.
   (1) Punic Wars.
   (2) Greece and Macedonia.
   (3) Beginnings of Literature.
   (*e*) Decay of the Republic, 146-46 B.C.

(1) The Gracchan disturbances, 130–121 B.C.
(2) Social War, 90 B.C.
(3) Marius and Sulla, 88 B.C.
(4) Pompey and Cáesar, 49 B.C.
(5) Progress of Literature.
(*f*) The Empire, 46 B.C.–476 A.D.—Decline of Political Life—General Prosperity—-Art and Literature.

LECTURE II.

SALIENT FEATURES OF ROMAN CHARACTER.

References.

Smith, Goldwin, The Greatness of the Romans, in Lectures and Essays, p. 1 ff.
Horace, Odes, iii, 1–6.
Wilkins, Primer of Roman Antiquities, chapter i.

1. The Romans contrasted with the Hebrews.
2. The Romans contrasted with the Greeks.
3. Positive traits :
   (*a*) Courage and steadfastness (*virtus et constantia*).
   (*b*) Practical character (*utilitas*).
   (*c*) Thriftiness and simplicity (*frugalitas*).
   (*d*) Love of formality and dignity (*gravitas, dignitas, severitas*).
   (*e*) Genius for organization—Legal sense.
   (*f*) Subordination of the individual to the state.
   (*g*) Cato viewed as a typical Roman.

LECTURE III.

GEOGRAPHY, CLIMATE, AND PRODUCTS OF ITALY.

References.[1]

Tozer, H. F., Classical Geography, in the series of Literature Primers, edited by J. R. Green.

[1] The references in this syllabus make no pretense at being a bibliography of the subject.

Jung, Julius,·Geographie und Geschichte des römischen Altertums, Part I. Geographie von Italien; in Müller's Handbuch der Klassischen Altertumswissenschaft, Band iii.

How and Leigh, History of Rome, Chap. i.

On climate and products, see Encyclopaedia Britannica, article Italy, pp. 441 ff.

A. Geography.

1. Three-fold division of Italy—Northern, Southern, Central—General characteristics—Coast line compared with Greece and Spain—Mountain ranges—No isolation as in Greece.

2. Northern Italy—Vast plain drained by Po and its tributaries.—Three subdivisions—Cis-Alpine Gaul, Venetia, Liguria—Mountains—Lakes.

3. Southern Italy—Extensive coast line—Few streams—Four subdivisions: Apulia, Calabria, Lucania, Bruttii.

4. Central Italy—Seven subdivisions: Etruria, Umbria, Sabine Territory, Picenum, Samnium, Campania ("The Crater"), Latium.

5. Latium—Level plain (Campagna)—Alban hills—Pontine Marshes—Rivers—Towns.

B. Climate.

1. Great differences in different sections—Three climatic zones, corresponding to the three geographical divisions—Differences between mountains and coast.

2. (*a*) Northern Italy—Temperate—Average temperature 55° (N. Y. 46°)—Riviera.

(*b*) Central Italy.—Average 58°.

(*c*) Southern Italy—Semi-tropical—Average 63°.

3. Malarial spots.

C. Products.

1. Vegetable—The staples: olive, wine, wheat, flax.

2. Animal—Cheese, honey, wool.

3. Mineral—Marble, some iron, copper.

LECTURE IV.

THE RACES OF ITALY.

References.

Mommsen, History of Rome (English translation), vol. i, chapters ii, iii, viii, ix, x.

How and Leigh, History of Rome, chapter ii.

Encyclopaedia Britannica, article Italy, p. 443 ff.

Jung, Julius, Geographie von Italien, in Müller's Handbuch der klassischen Altertumswissenschaft, vol. iii, pp. 472 ff.

Niese, Bernard, Römische Geschichte, in Müller's Handbuch, vol. iii, pp. 580–584.

A. Indo-European Races.

1. Original home of the Indo-European family.
2. Italic group.
    (a) Latin tribes : Romans (Volsci, Aequi?).
    (b) Umbro-Samnitic tribes.
        (1) Umbrians.
        (2) Sabini.
        (3) Marsi, Vestini, Marrucini, Paeligni, Frentani, Picentini.
        (4) Samnites.
        (5) Lucani.
        (6) Bruttii.
3. Gauls.
    (a) Insubres.
    (b) Senones.
4. Greeks.—In Magna Graecia.
5. Veneti (?).

B. Non-Indo-European Races.

1. Etruscans.
2. Iapygians.
3. Ligurians.

PART I.

TOPOGRAPHY AND REMAINS OF ANCIENT ROME.

LECTURE V.

GENERAL TOPOGRAPHY OF THE CITY OF ROME.—THE
EARLY REMAINS.

References.

Middleton, J. H., Ancient Rome,[1] vol. 1, chapters iii–iv.

Lanciani, Rodolfo, Ruins and Excavations of Ancient Rome, Book i.

—— ——, Ancient Rome in the Light of Recent Discoveries,
chapter ii.

Richter, Otto, article 'Rom' in Baumeister's Denkmäler des
klassischen Altertums.

—— ——, Topographie der Stadt Rom, in Müller's Handbuch der
klassischen Altertumswissenschaft, Band iii, p. 716 ff.

Schneider, A., Das alte Rom, Tafeln i–iii, and Plans at end.

Kiepert and Hülsen, Forma Urbis Romae Antiquae, Map I in pocket
at end.

Burn, R., Ancient Rome and its Neighbourhood, p. 1 ff.

Ramsay, W., Manual of Roman Antiquities, pp. 1–14.

Burn, Rome and the Campagna, chapters i, iii, iv, v.

Photographs 10.003, 10.004, 10.071, 17.010, 32.045.

1. Topography of Rome and vicinity—Volcanic origin of
the hills—Their richness in building material—Importance
of this.

2. Six stages in the topographical development of Rome.

(*a*) Palatium.

(*b*) Septimontium.

(*c*) City of the 'Four Regions.'

(*d*) The Wall and Agger of Servius.

---

[1] The earlier editions of this work in one volume may also be consulted.

(*e*) The Open city of Fourteen Regions under Augustus.
(*f*) The Aurelian Wall.

3. Existing remains of the early periods: "Walls of Romulus"—Wall and Agger of Servius—Cloaca Maxima—Other cloacae—The river embankment—Tullianum—Carcer.

4. Subsequent architectural eras of Rome.
(*a*) Augustus, 30 B.C.–14 A.D.
(*b*) Nero, 54–68 A.D.
(*c*) The Flavian dynasty, 69–96 A.D.
(*d*) Trajan, 98–117 A.D.
(*e*) Hadrian, 117–138 A.D.
(*f*) Septimius Severus and Caracalla, 193–217 A.D.
(*g*) Aurelian, 274 A.D.
(*h*) Constantine, 306–337 A.D.

LECTURE VI.

THE ROMAN FORUM.

References.

Middleton, J. H., Ruins of Ancient Rome, vol. i, chapters vi, vii.
Lanciani, R., Ruins and Excavations, Book iii, p. 216 ff.
—— ——, Ancient Rome in the Light of Recent Discoveries, chapters iv, vi.
Ramsay, W., Manual of Roman Antiquities, pp. 15–35.
Baedeker, Karl, Guide Book to Central Italy, p. 217 ff.
Strack, H., Die Baudenkmäler des alten Rom, p. 20 and Plates 1, 2, 8, 16, 21, 22.
Parker, J. H., Forum Romanum (gives illustrations of early state of F.)
Hülsen, Das Forum Romanum, Plates.
Burn, Rome and the Campagna, chapter vi, part i; chapter vi, part ii.
Burn, Ancient Rome and its Neighborhood, p. 41 ff.
Photographs: A, B, C; 18.015, 98.072 ff.

1. Historical importance of the locality.

2. State of the Forum in the Middle Ages—Stages in its excavation.

3. The original site—Made available by drainage—*Tabernae* of Tarquinius Priscus.

4. Curia—Comitium Rostra—Umbilicus Romae—Milliarium Aureum.

5. Temple of Saturn—Basilica Julia—Temple of Castor.

6. Temple of Vesta—Atrium Vestae—Temple of Julius Cæsar—Temple of Antoninus and Faustina.

7. Temple of Concord—Temple of Vespasian—Arch of Septimius Severus.

8. Central Area—Reliefs of Trajan—Bases of Honorary Columns—Column of Phocas.

9. Sacra Via—The Unexcavated Environs.

LECTURE VII.

THE IMPERIAL FORA.

References.

Middleton, J. H., Ruins of Ancient Rome, vol. ii, chapter i.

Lanciani, R., Ruins and Excavations, See Index on p. 598 f.

—— ——, Ancient Rome in the Light of Recent Discoveries, chapter iv.

Ramsay, Manual of Roman Antiquities, pp. 35–39.

Baedeker, Karl, Central Italy, p. 233 ff.

Strack, H., Baudenkmäler des alten Rom, Plates 7, 15, 26, 29.

Schneider, Das Alte Rom, Tafel vi, No. 12 ; vii, No. 11.

Cichorius, C., Die Reliefs der Trajanssäule, (Plates).

Baumeister, Denkmäler, see Index under Trajanssäule.

Burn, Rome and the Campagna, chapter vii.

——, Ancient Rome, p. 100 ff.

Photographs : D ; 18.040, 18.041, 18.051, 18.060, 18.061, 20.025-27.

1. The Forum Julium—Temple of Venus Genetrix.

2. Forum Augusti—Temple of Mars Ultor.

3. Forum or Templum Pacis—Vespasian.

4. Forum Nervae (Forum Transitorium)—Temple of Minerva.

5. Forum of Trajan—Extent of the excavations for its construction—Basilica Ulpia—Trajan's Column—Temple of Trajan.

LECTURE VIII.

THE CAPITOLINE AND THE PALATINE.

References.

Middleton, Ancient Rome, vol. i, chapters iv, viii.
Lanciani, Ruins and Excavations, Book ii ; also p. 296 ff.
——, Ancient Rome in the Light of Recent Discoveries, chapter v.
Ramsay, W., Manual of Roman Antiquities, pp. 39–46.
Baedeker, Karl, Central Italy, p. 208 ff. ; 237 ff.
Burn, Rome and the Campagna, chapter viii, part i, part ii.
——, Ancient Rome, p. 120 ff. ; p. 13 ff.
Photographs : E, F ; 32.038, 32.050, 32.060, 32.062.

1. The Capitoline—Arx and Temple of Juno Moneta—Capitolium — Temple of Jupiter Capitolinus — Tarpeian Rock—Inter Duos Lucos.

2. The Palatine—Succession of Palaces—Augustus, Tiberius, Caligula, (Nero ?)—Flavian Emperors—Septizonium —Temple of Apollo ; the Palatine Library (27 B.C.).

LECTURE IX.

OTHER IMPORTANT STRUCTURES.

References.

Middleton, Ancient Rome, vol. ii, chapter ix, and see Index.
Lanciani, Ruins and Excavations, see Index.
——, Atlantic Monthly, vol. lxxi, p. 721 (on the Pantheon).
Ramsay, W., Manual of Roman Antiquities, see Index.
Strack, H., Baudenkmäler des alten Rom, Plates, 3–6 ; 12–14 ; 18, 20, 23, 32.
Schneider, Das alte Rom ; see Tafeln *passim.*
Burn, Rome and the Campagna ; see Index.
Burn, Ancient Rome, p. 159 ff.
Baedeker, Central Italy ; see Index.
Byron, Childe Harold, Canto iv, Stanza cxlvi f.
Photographs : G, H, I, J, K, L, M, N ; 10.042, 19.010, 19.011, 19.014, 19.025, 19.030, 19.040, 19.041.

1. Pantheon—Agrippa—27 B.C.

2. Triumphal and other Arches.

(*a*) Titus—the reliefs—capture of Jerusalem, 70 A.D.

(*b*) Constantine, 325 A.D.

(*c*) Drusus.

(*d*) Janus Quadrifrons.

3. Column of Marcus Aurelius (176 A.D.)—Temple of Fortuna Virilis—Temple of Hercules—Temple of Venus and Rome—Basilica of Constantine.

PART II.

PRIVATE ANTIQUITIES.

LECTURE X.

MARRIAGE, STATUS OF WOMEN, CELIBACY, DIVORCE.

References.

Ramsay, Manual of Roman Antiquities, p. 293 ff. ; 477 ff.
Preston and Dodge, Private Life of the Romans, pp. 8–17.
Maine, Sir Henry, Ancient Law, chapter v, *Patria Potestas.*
Wilkins, Primer of Roman Antiquities, chapter iv.
Inge, W. R., Society in Rome under the Cæsars, chapter vii.
Becker's Gallus, p. 153 ff.
Smith[1], Dictionary of Antiquities, article *matrimonium.*
Marquardt, Das Privatleben der Römer, pp. 28–80.
Zoeller, Römische Privataltertümer, p. 204 ff.
Friedländer, Darstellungen aus der Sittengeschichte Roms,[5] vol. i,
chapter v.
Catullus, Carmen lxi.

1. Qualifications necessary to a valid marriage—Political
—Age—Nearness of relationship.

2. Origin and significance of *patria potestas.*

3. Marriage with *manus*—Without *manus.*

4. Betrothal—Wedding ceremonies—Their religious character—Different methods of marriage *in manum: confar-
reatio; usus; coemtio*—Special significance of these.

5. Status of woman—Her freedom and dignity—Contrast
with conditions at Athens.

6. Changes in the character of the Roman matron under
the later Republic and Empire.

7. Divorce—Originally rare—Increasing frequency in
later times—Causes.

8. Celibacy—Causes—Fruitless attempts to check it by
legislation.

---

[1] All references to Smith apply also to Harper's Classical Dictionary.

LECTURE XI.

CHILDREN, THEIR LEGAL STATUS, CEREMONIES AT AND AFTER BIRTH.

References.

Ramsay, Manual, p. 475 ff.
Preston and Dodge, Private Life, p. 57 ff.
Wilkins, Primer, chapter iv.
Becker, Gallus, p. 178 ff.
Smith, Dictionary, under *susceptio, bulla, dies lustricus, crepundia.*
Inge, Society in Rome, p. 69 ff.
Marquardt, Privatleben, p. 81 ff.
Zoeller, Römische Privataltertümer, p. 219 ff.

1. Exposure of children—*patria potestas*—*susceptio*—Cruel treatment of foundlings.
2. Religious ceremonies at the birth of children—*primordia*—*dies lustricus*—*crepundia*—*fascinatio*—*bulla aurea*—*bulla scortea.*
3. Tutelary deities of children.
4. Registration of births—*professio.*

LECTURE XII.

ROMAN NAMES.

References.

Ramsay, Manual, p. 88 ff. ; 125 ; 131.
Smith, Dictionary, under *nomen.*
Preston and Dodge, Private Life ; see Index.
Marquardt, Privatleben, p. 7 ff.
Zöller, Römische Privataltertümer, p. 222 ff.

A. Men's Names.

1. Three periods.
   (*a*) Original method,—single name, e. g. *Lucius.*
   (*b*) Early historical period,—two names, e. g. *Lucius Quinctius.*

(*c*) Later historical period—three names (the normal method), e. g. *Lucius Quinctius Cincinnatus.*

2. *Praenomen*, *nomen*, *cognomen*, *agnomen*—Paucity of *praenomina*—Inversion of *nomen* and *cognomen.*

B. Women's Names.

Four stages :
  (*a*) One name, e. g. *Gaia* (*Luci*).
  (*b*) Two names, e. g. *Gaia Cornelia.*
  (*c*) Gentile name alone, e. g. *Cornelia.*
  (*d*) Gentile and family name, e. g. *Cornelia Scipio.*

C. Slaves' Names.

Three stages :
  (*a*) Designated by master's name. e. g. *Marcipor.*
  (*b*) Individual names, mostly foreign, e. g. *Aphrodisius.*
  (*c*) Individual name followed by master's name in the genitive.

D. Freedmen's Names.

First two names of master followed by the slave name.

E.

Breaking down of Roman system of names under the Empire.

LECTURE XIII.

EARLY LIFE, SPORTS, AND EDUCATION OF ROMAN CHILDREN.

References.

Wilkins, Primer, chapter iv.
Preston and Dodge, Private Life. p. 57 f.
Becker, Gallus, p. 182 ff.
Ramsay, W., Manual, p. 475 f.
Smith, Dictionary, under Education.
Clarke, Geo., Education of Children at Rome.

Laurie, S. S., Roman Education, in School Review, vol. iii, p. 143 ff. ; p. 211 ff.

Marquardt, Privatleben, p. 81 ff.

Zoeller, Römische Altertümer, p. 230 ff.

Photographs : 52.030, 52.040, 81.010.

1. Games of children—Existence at Rome of modern games—Nut-games—Ball-games—Their simplicity.

2. Training of children—Theory of Roman education,—practical, to subserve the public welfare (Greek education individual and ideal)—Strong home influences at Rome—The mother.

3. Formal instruction.

(a) Elementary—' The Three R's '—Teachers: the *litterator* and *calculator*—Small fees—Long terms—Holidays—The *paedagogus*.

(b) Grammatical (*i. e.*, literary)—Our high school—Study of Greek and Latin authors—The *grammaticus*.

(c) Rhetorical—In rhetoric and oratory—Modelled on Greek plan — Lectures by teacher — Exercises by pupils—Declamation—*Controversiae* and *Suasoriae*.

4. Higher education—Absence of facilities for specialization—The philosophical schools—Foreign study—Hadrian's universities.

5. Instruction of girls—Essentially domestic.

6. Assumption of toga virilis—Ceremonies—Consequences —*Tirocinium*.

LECTURE XIV.

SLAVES, THEIR STATUS, EMPLOYMENT, AND TREATMENT.

References.

Wilkins, Primer, chapter iv.

Preston and Dodge, Private Life, pp. 66–72.

Ramsay, W., Manual, p. 124 ff.

Inge, Society in Rome, p. 159 ff.

Smith, Dictionary, under *servus, peculium*.

Becker, Gallus, p. 199 ff.

Marquardt, Privatleben, p. 135 ff.
Zoeller, Römische Altertümer, p. 245 ff.

1. Importance of Roman slavery—Causes of increase in number of slaves.
2. *Familia rustica*—Agricultural and pastoral pursuits.
3. *Familia urbana*—
    (*a*) Management of house.
    (*b*) Personal attendance.
    (*c*) Cuisine.
    (*d*) Table-service.
    (*e*) Escort about the city.
    (*f*) Clerical and literary service.
4. Management, care, and education of slaves—*paedagogia*.
5. Number of slaves—Chiefly employed in agricultural and industrial occupations.
6. Sources of supply.
    (*a*) Captives in war.
    (*b*) By kidnapping.
    (*c*) From foreign slave-markets.
    (*d*) By legal process.
    (*e*) By birth in house of master (*vernae*).—Slave-trade controlled by aediles—Prices.
7. Treatment of slaves—Slave marriages—*peculium*—Harsh treatment toward close of republic—Modes of punishment.
8. Amelioration of condition of slaves under Empire—Causes.

LECTURE XV.

FREEDMEN, GUEST-FRIENDS, CLIENTS.

References.

Wilkins, Primer, chapter iii.
Preston and Dodge, p. 72 ff.
Becker, Gallus, p. 226 ff.
Ramsay, W., Manual, see Index under *hospites, clientes, liberti.*

Inge, Society in Rome ; see chapter vi.
Smith, Dictionary, under *hospitium, cliens, sportula, libertus.*
Marquardt, Privatleben, p. 195 ff.
Zoeller, Römische Altertümer, p. 255 ff.

1. Modes of manumission—Political status of *liberti*—Social status.

2. Guest-friends—Antiquity of the institution—Definiteness of obligation—Cities as guest-friends.

3. Client and patron—Obligations mutual—Recognized legal character—Clients originally plebeians.

4. Changed clientship of the later Republic and Empire—A purely voluntary relation—Artificial character—The sportula—Decline of independence.

LECTURE XVI.

THE ROMAN HOUSE.

References.

Preston and Dodge, Private Life, p. 28 ff.
Wilkins, Primer, chapter ii.
Ramsay, Manual, p. 516.
Smith, Dictionary, under *Domus.*
Bulwer-Lytton, Last Days of Pompeii, chapter iii.
Guhl and Koner, Life of the Greeks and Romans, p. 357 ff.
Becker, Gallus, p. 231 ff.
Overbeck, Pompeii, chapter iv.
Marquardt, Privatleben, p. 213.
Zoeller, Römische Altertümer, p. 267 ff.
Photographs : 77.005, 12.045, 12.050, 13.050, 60.010, 60.012, 60.016, 60.025, 60.030, 60.034, 60.040, 60.070, 61.005, 61.050, 61.070.

1. Scanty remains of houses at Rome—But one or two specimens preserved—Pompeii the source of our knowledge.

2. Fundamental difference between ancient and modern houses found in the method of securing light—Romans lacked glass.

3. The Roman house a development from one room,—the *atrium*—Proofs of this—Etymology of *atrium*—The *compluvium* and *impluvium*.

4. Steps in the extension of the *atrium* :—*alae, tablinum,.
peristyle, hortus.*
5. General adherence to type—Free variation in detail.
6. *Sacraria (lararia).*

_____.____

LECTURE XVII.

HOUSEHOLD DECORATION, FURNITURE, AND UTENSILS.

References.

Preston and Dodge, Private Life, p. 39 f.
Guhl and Koner, Life of the Greeks and Romans, p. 437 ff.
Overbeck, Pompeii, chapter v.
Becker, Gallus, p. 285 ff.
Smith, Dictionary, under *Domus.*
Marquardt, Privatleben, p. 646 ff.
Zöller, Privataltertümer, p. 281 ff.
Baumeister, Denkmäler, under Pompeii.
Photographs : 46.020, 46.030, 46.031, 46.032, 62, 66, 67, 69, 70, 71,
72, 73, 74, 75, 92.025, 94.001, 98.042—052.

A. Decoration.

1. Wall Paintings.
2. Mosaics.

B. Furniture.

1. Small variety of Roman furniture as compared with
modern standards—Scanty remains of wooden furniture at
Pompeii.
2. Beds.—Bedsteads probably uncommon—No samples
preserved—Usually built in—Wash-stands—Often of stone.
3. Seats —Often of stone or bronze—*bisellia.*
4. Tables—Marble stands—Tripods—Tetrapods—Artistic
designs.
5. Lamps — Candelabra — Lanterns — Imperfection of
ancient lighting—No chimneys—Sooty deposits.

C. Utensils.

1. Ovens—Portable furnaces—Braziers.

2. Kitchen Utensils : Skillets, strainers, kettles, ladles.
3. Pottery—Glass-ware—Spoons—Knives.
4. Axes—Hatchets—Spades—Steelyards—Sundials (*horologia, solaria*)—Reckoning of time—Clepsydras.
5. Keys—Knockers—Draw-pulls.

LECTURE XVIII.

MEALS, FOOD, DRINK.

References.

Becker's Gallus, p. 451 ff.; 476 ff.; 485 ff.
Wilkins, Primer, chapter iii.
Preston and Dodge, Private Life, p. 77.
Ramsay, Manual, p. 490 ff.
Guhl and Koner, Life of the Greeks and Romans, p. 501.
Marquardt, Privatleben, p. 414 f.
Zoeller, Privataltertümer, p. 289.
Inge, Society at Rome, p. 196 ; 202 ; 262.
Horace, *Sat.* ii, 8.

1. Names and order of meals—At first *jentaculum, cena, vesperna ;* later *jentaculum, prandium, cena.*
2. The *cena :*
   (*a*) *gustus (gustatio),*
   (*b*) *fercula,*
   (*c*) *mensae secundae.*
3. Table customs—Reclining at table (*accumbere, discumbere*)—The *triclinium*—The *lecti* : *medius, summus, imus*—*Sigma* or *stibadium*—*Umbrae.*
4. The table—Knives and forks lacking—Spoons used— Napkins and table-cloths a late luxury—Platters.
5. The Comissatio (συμπόσιον) — *Magister bibendi* — *Nomen bibere.*
6. Food—Simple in early time—Later more elaborate.
   (*a*) Fish—Extravagant taste of Romans for this— Enormous prices—Mullets, lampreys, etc.
   (*b*) Fowl—Peacock, pheasant, etc.
   (*c*) Beef little used—Pork, game, boar, hare.

(*d*) Vegetables and fruits in great variety.

(*e*) Oil, cheese, honey, pastry.

7. Drinks—Wine the staple—Beer, spirits, and decoctions unknown.

8. The public grain supply.

9. Roman luxury.

XIX.

DRESS OF MEN AND WOMEN.

References.

Preston and Dodge, Private Life, p. 95.
Wilkins, Primer, chapter iv.
Becker, Gallus, p. 408 ff.
Ramsay, Manual, p. 504 ff.
Guhl and Koner, Life of the Greeks and Romans, p. 476 ff.
Smith, Dictionary under *toga, calceus.*
Baumeister, Denkmäler, under *Toga, Fussbekleidung.*
Weiss, Kostümkunde, I, p. 957.
Marquardt, Privatleben, p. 550.
Zoeller, Römische Privataltertümer, p. 298.
Photographs 81.024 ff., 81.070 ff.

1. Dress of men—*subucula—tunica—toga.*

2. The toga—Styles of wearing—*sinus—umbo—cinctus Gabinus*—at sacrifices—*toga picta*—Material of toga—Color.

3. *Paenula, sagum, lacerna.*

4. Dress of women—*tunica interior—stola—palla—tunico-pallium.*

5. Footwear—*calcei* (shoes)—*soleae* (sandals).

6. Headgear—Less used than by us—*pileus, petasus.*

7. Men's hair—The beard—*tondere, radere*—Wigs.

8. Women's hair—Elaborate coiffures—False hair.

9. Jewelry and ornaments—Rings, bracelets, brooches—Mirrors, fans, *etc.*

LECTURE XX.

BATHS AND AQUEDUCTS.

References.

Becker, Gallus, p. 366.
Lanciani, Ancient Rome, p. 49.
——, Ruins and Excavations ; see Index.
Guhl and Koner, Life of the Greeks and Romans, p. 351 ; 396.
Ramsay, Manual, p. 487 ; 78–84.
Parker, J. H., The Aqueducts of Rome (with admirable illustrations).
Middleton, Ancient Rome, vol. ii, chapters v, x.
Wilkins, Primer, p. 38.
Preston and Dodge, Private Life, p. 48.
Smith, Dictionary, under *balneae, etc.*
Baumeister, Denkmäler, under Thermen.
Marquardt, Privatleben, p. 269.
Parker, J. H., Archaeology of Rome, vol. viii.
Herschel, Clemens, Frontinus and his Two Books on the Water Supply of the City of Rome.
Strack, Baudenkmäler des alten Rom, Plates 28, 33.
Photographs : O, P ; 10.041, 15.010, 15.011, 15.015, 15.016, 15.018, 15.030, 15.040, 15.060, 16.005, 16.060, 31.030, 31.040, 31.041, 31.050, 31.060, 31.070, 31.090, 31.095, 86, 68.020–68.090.

1. Baths, foreign origin—*balneae, thermae*—The latter modelled on the Greek gymnasium.

2. The important *thermae* at Rome—of Agrippa, of Titus, Trajan, Caracalla, Diocletian, Constantine.

3. The Baths at Pompeii.

4. Description of one of the great *thermae—apodyterium, elaiothesium, tepidarium, calidarium, frigidarium, Laconicon, hypocausts, suspensurae*—The service—Athletic grounds — Dining rooms, libraries, *etc.*

5. Aqueducts—Earliest aqueducts entirely subterranean —Later ones built partly on arches—Principles of construction—Fall not pressure—Enormous length—*Castella*—Distributing mains—List of chief Roman aqueducts.

6. Aqueducts outside of Rome.

7. Fountains.

LECTURE XXI.

THE CIRCENSIAN GAMES.

References.

Wilkins, Primer, p. 93.
Guhl and Koner, Life of the Greeks and Romans, p. 422 ff. ; 546 ff.
Ramsay, Manual, p. 394 f.
Richter, Spiele der Griechen und Romer, p. 152.
Lanciani, Ancient Rome ; see Index under Circus Maximus.
Inge, Society in Rome, p. 216 ff.
Middleton, Ancient Rome, vol. ii, chapter ii.
Lanciani, Ruins and Excavations ; see Index under *Circus*.
Friedländer Sittengeschichte[5] ii, p. 283.
Baumeister, Denkmäler, under *Cirkus*.
Smith, Dictionary, under *Circus, Circenses*.
Wallace, Ben Hur, book v, chapter xiv.
Burn, Rome and the Campagna, p. 295 ff.
Zoeller, Privataltertümer, p. 379 ff.
Photographs : 29.005, 29.050, 88.

1. The Circus Maximus—Location—Size—2000 x 600 feet—150,000–385,000 spectators—*spina*—*metae*—Eggs and dolphins—*carceres*—*calx*—*pulvinar*—Circus of Maxentius.

2. Early religious character of the Circensian Games— Imposing ceremonial—The presiding official.

3. The races—Four chariots—Four or two horses—Seven laps (*missus*)—Number of races—The jockeys—Colors and factions : red, white, blue, green—Political significance of these—Pay of the jockeys.

4. Increased frequency of the games under the Empire— Passion of the Romans for them—"*panem et Circenses.*"

LECTURE XXII.

THE GAMES OF THE AMPHITHEATRE.

References.

Middleton, Ancient Rome, vol. ii, chapter iv.
Smith, Dictionary, under Coliseum, Gladiators.
Wilkins, Primer, p. 103.

Parker, J. H., Coliseum.
Richter, Spiele der Griechen und Römer, p. 173 ff.
Ramsay, Manual, p. 404-409.
Guhl and Koner, Life of the Greeks and Romans, p. 553 ff.
Burn, Rome and the Campagna, p. 234 ff.
——, Ancient Rome, p. 71 ff.
Friedländer, Sittengeschichte,[5] ii, p. 318 ff.
Inge, Society in Rome, p. 53 ff. ; 210 ff.
Baumeister, Denkmäler, under Amphitheater.
Post, American Journal of Philology, vol. xiii, p. 213.
Strack, Baudenkmäler des alten Rom, Plates 9-11.
Lanciani, Ruins and Excavations, p. 367.
Zoeller, Privataltertümer, p. 384 ff.
Byron, Childe Harold, Canto iv, Stanza cxlii ff.
Photographs : Q, R, S ; 27.005, 27.010, 27.015, 27.020, 27.025, 27.030, 89.

1. Coliseum—Origin of the name—Its Roman name *Amphitheatrum Flavium*—Vespasian and Titus, 80 A.D.— Three stories—Later four—Capacity 100,000—*arena*— *podium*—The seats—Four tiers—Canopies—Masts—Substructures.

2. Gladiatorial contests—Fought in Coliseum and other amphitheatres—Gladiatorial schools—Severity of the training.

3. Classes of gladiators—*retiarii*, *mirmillones*, Sabines, Thracians—Weapons, and modes of fighting—Character of the contests—Conditions of mercy—*pollice verso*.

4. Contests with wild beasts.

5. Sham naval fights—*naumachiae.*

6. Boxing.

LECTURE XXIII.

THEATRES.

References.

Middleton, Ancient Rome, vol. ii, chapter iii.
Lanciani, Ruins and Excavations, see Index under Theatres.
Baumeister, Denkmäler, p. 1757.
Friedländer, Sittengeschichte,[5] ii, p. 391 ff.
Marquardt, Staatsverwaltung, vol. iii, p. 528.

Zöller, Privataltertümer, p. 389 ff.
Ramsay, Manual, p. 59 f.; 401 ff.
Strack, Baudenkmäler des alten Rom, Plate 25.
Photographs : 87.

1. Early prejudice against permanent theatres at Rome—
Theatre of Pompey—Theatre of Marcellus.
2. Details of construction—*cavea, cunei, aulaeum, orches-tra.*
3. Early disappearance of legitimate drama at Rome—
Roman love of the spectacular.
4. Successors of tragedy :
   (*a*) Pantomimes, *i. e.*, acting of striking scenes from
   familiar tragic legends—Gesticulation prominent—A
   simple text chanted by chorus—Immoral tendencies.
   (*b*) Dramatic songs—Nero's famous rôle.
5. *Atellanae* and *Mimi.*
6. Ballet dancing—*Pyrrhicha.*
7. Social position of actors at Rome—Pecuniary compen-
sations—Factions—Tumults.

LECTURE XXIV.

BOOKS, AUTHORS, RECITATIONS, PUBLISHERS, LIBRARIES, CORRESPONDENCE, SHORTHAND, NEWS-PAPERS, THE POST.

References.

Preston and Dodge, Private Life, p. 36.
Putnam, G. H., Books and their Public in Ancient Times, chapter v.
Guhl and Koner, Life of the Greeks and Romans, p. 529.
Becker, Gallus, p. 325 ff.
Lanciani, Ancient Rome, chapter vii.
Birt, Das Antike Buchwesen.
Marquardt, Privatleben, p. 799 ff.
Zöller, Privataltertümer, p. 349 ff.

1. Materials and construction of the book—Papyrus—Its
Preparation—Parchment—Leather—Other materials—Ink—
Pens—The roll (*volumen*)—*Umbilicus*—Pages—*Scrinia*—
Titles—*Opisthographa—The Codex.*

2. Publication—Multiplication of copies by dictation—Arrangements with authors—Royalties—Size of editions—Prices of copies—Publishers—Book-shops.

3. The recitation—Way of introducing new works to the public.

4. Libraries.

5. Note-books and correspondence—Use of wax-tablets (*pugillares*) —*Stilus*—Amanuenses—Shorthand.

6. Newspapers.

7. Postal system.

LECTURE XXV.

ARTS AND INDUSTRIES.

References.

Marquardt, Privatleben, Theil II, chaps. 3, 4.
Göll, Culturbilder, i, p. 162.
Preston and Dodge, Private Life, p. 105.
Guhl u. Koner, Life of the Greeks and Romans, p. 519-533.
Zöller, Privataltertümer, p. 340 ff.
Photographs : 94.015-.018, 94.066 ff., 95.

1. Contempt of the Romans for industrial occupations, except farming.

2. Organization of Roman artisans into guilds (*collegia*)—Tutelary divinities.

3. Classification of industries :

A. Manual Industries.

(*a*) Farming and cattle-raising—Bee-keeping—Fish culture.

(*b*) Wine-making.

(*c*) Milling and baking.

(*d*) Fulling and dyeing.

(*e*) Pottery.

(*f*) Metal-work.

(*g*) Glass.

B. Learned Professions.

(*a*) Teachers.
(*b*) Physicians.
(*c*) Lawyers.
(*d*) Artists.

LECTURE XXVI.

DEATH AND BURIAL.

References.

Becker, Gallus, p. 505.
Guhl and Koner, Life of the Greeks and Romans, p. 377 ff., 591 ff.
Preston and Dodge, Private Life, p. 17.
Smith, Dictionary of antiquities, under *columbarium, funus.*
Marquardt, Privatleben, Theil i. Abschnitt viii.
Göll, Culturbilder, ii, p. 326.
Baumeister, Denkmäler, p. 308.
Zoeller, Privataltertümer, p. 323 ff.
Middleton, Ancient Rome, vol. ii, chapter viii.
Byron, Childe Harold, Canto iv, Stanza xcix ff. ; clii.
Photographs : T, U, V, W ; 11.050, 11.051, 11.052, 98.045 ff.,99.072 ff.

1. Death—The *conclamatio.*
2. Funeral ceremonies—Undertakers (*libitinarii*)—Hired mourners (*praeficae*)—The funeral procession—Ancestral *imagines*—Funeral oration (*laudatio*).
5. Disposition of the body—Regularly outside the walls.
   (*a*) Interment.
      (1) In sarcophagi and tombs.
      (2) In the ground—poorer classes.
   (*b*) Cremation.
      (1) The *bustum*—burning over an open grave.
      (2) The *rogus* or funeral pyre—*Ustrina*—Ashes gathered in urns.
4. Funeral feasts—Services in commemoration of the dead—*novemdial—parentalia.*
5. Funeral monuments.
   (*a*) Tombs, *e. g.,* of the Scipios.
   (*b*) *Columbaria.*

(*c*) Special memorials—Tomb of Caecilia Metella—
Mausoleum of Hadrian—Pyramid of Cestius—Street
of Tombs at Pompeii.

LECTURE XXVII.

BELIEF OF THE ROMANS IN IMMORTALITY.

References.

Friedländer, Sittengeschichte[5], iii, p. 681–716.
Boissier, La Religion Romaine, vol. i, p. 263 ff.

A. Views of the Educated Classes.

1. Opponents of the doctrine—Pliny the Elder—The
Epicureans.
2. Arguments in favor of immortality (Plato).
3. The Stoic view—Immortality for a limited period—
Seneca—Striking resemblance to Christian teaching.

B. Views of the Uneducated Classes.

1. General belief in immortality.
2. Belief in the Greek mythological conceptions of the
environment and occupation of souls after death—Materi-
alistic character of these views.
3. Belief in shades and apparitions as a ground for the
belief in immortality.

C. Contrast between the Roman and Christian Conceptions of the Future Life.

1. The Christian faith, a revelation—The Roman a result
of experience.
2. Clear connection between the dead and living to the
Roman mind.
3. Relatively greater importance attached by the Romans
to the present life.

PART III.

PUBLIC ANTIQUITIES.

LECTURE XXVIII.

INTRODUCTORY.

1. Plan and scope.
2. Bibliography.

LECTURE XXIX.

HISTORY OF THE REGAL PERIOD.

References.

Ihne, W., Early Rome, chapters ii–iv.
————, History of Rome, vol. i, book i, chapters i–xii.
How and Leigh, History of Rome, pp. 20–40.
Allen, Short History of the Roman People, p. 13 ff.
Tighe, A., Development of the Roman Constitution, chapter i.
Granrud, J. E., Roman Constitutional History, First Period.

I. Character of Early Roman History.

1. Views of the Romans themselves as to the credibility of their early history.

2. Beginnings of modern criticism—Vico, Pouilly, Beaufort, 1725–1750.

3. Niebuhr—*Roman History*—1811—Shows mythological and legendary character of early history.

4. Lewis—*Credibility of Early Roman History*, 1855.

5. Grounds of Niebuhr's views.
    (*a*) Lack of contemporary evidence—Earliest annalists 200 B.C.
    (*b*) Untrustworthy character of oral tradition—Influence of family pride.

(c) Internal inconsistencies.

(d) Chronological difficulties—Extraordinary duration of the reign of the Kings.

(e) Moral impossibilities—Institutions of Numa.

(f) Traces of late borrowing under Greek influence— Story of Sextus Tarquinius—Brutus's mission to Delphi. .

II. Reconstruction of History of Regal Period.

1. Rome a Latin settlement.

2. The original city a small fortified enclosure on the Palatine.

3. Amalgamation with the Sabines.

4. The original monarchy sacerdotal.

5. Overthrow of the sacerdotal monarchy ; establishment of the military monarchy (an Etruscan conquest ?).

LECTURE XXX.

ORGANIZATION OF THE ROMAN STATE IN THE REGAL PERIOD.

References.

Ihne, Early Rome, chapters v–ix.
——, History of Rome, vol. i, book i, chapter xiii.
Mommsen, History of Rome, vol. i, chapters v, vi.
How and Leigh, History of Rome, pp. 40–47.
Ramsay, Manual, p. 165, 87–93 ; 147–150.
Zöller, Römische Staatsaltertümer, pp. 154–167 ; 8–26 ; 73–79.
Tighe, Roman Constitution, chapter iii.
Allen, Short History, pp. 18–37.
Gow, Companion to School Classics, pp. 164–169.
Granrud, Roman Constitutional History, First Period.

A. The King.

1. Mode of Appointment—*interrex—decuriae—auctoritas patrum—lex curiata.*

2. Powers and functions of the King.
    (*a*) Executive—Commander in wars—Oversight of religion.
    (*b*) Judicial.
    (*c*) Legislative.

3. Emoluments and insignia of the king : *trabea*, sceptre, lictors.

4. Assistants of the King: *praefectus urbi* ; *quaestores* ; *duumviri*—Sacerdotal assistants ; *flamens, augurs, etc.*

B. The Senate.

1. Membership—100–300.

2. Functions — Representative and advisory — *auctoritas patrum*—Absence of legislative powers.

C. The People.

1. The different orders.
    (*a*) Before Servius Tullius : citizens, clients.
    (*b*) After Servius Tullius—The Plebeians.

2. Organization of the People.
    (*a*) Before Servius Tullius—The *Curiae.*
    (*b*) Servius's reforms—Tribes, classes, centuries.

3. The political functions of the people—The Comitia Curiata.

LECTURE XXXI.

SKETCH OF THE CONSTITUTIONAL HISTORY OF REPUBLI-
CAN ROME FROM THE EXPULSION OF THE KINGS TO
THE EQUALIZATION OF THE ORDERS (510–367 B.C.)

References.

Ihne, History of Rome, vol. i, pp. 127–334.
How and Leigh, History of Rome, pp. 47–94.
Fowler, W. W., The City–State, chapters vii, viii.
Allen, Short History, pp. 38–76.
Granrud, Roman Constitutional History, Second Period, chapters i–v.

1. Constitutional significance of the establishment of the Republic—The consuls as compared with the kings.

2. General features of the period from 510-367 B.C.— Gradual advance of the plebeians to full political equality.

3. Grievances of plebeians :
   (a) Unjust laws regarding debtors.
   (b) Unfair administration of laws in general.
   (c) Mal-administration of public lands.

4. The first secession of the plebs (494 B.C.)—Institution of tribunes and of the *concilium plebis*.

5. The Terentilian Rogations (462 B.C.)—Plebeians demand a code—The Decemvirate (450 B.C.)—Laws of the Twelve Tables—The Second Secession (449 B.C.)—Valerio-Horatian laws.

6. Canuleian Law (445 B.C.)—Right of intermarriage.

7. Institution of consular tribunes (445 B.C.).

8. Establishment of the censorship (443 B.C.)—The quaestorship opened to plebeians (421 B.C.).

9. Plebeians first elect consular tribunes in 400 B.C.

10. The Licinian Rogations (367 B.C.).

LECTURE XXXII.

CONSTITUTIONAL HISTORY OF REPUBLICAN ROME FROM THE LICINIAN ROGATIONS TO THE GRACCHI (367-133 B.C.).

References.

How and Leigh, History of Rome, pp. 93-97 ; and chapters xxviii, xxix.

Allen, Short History, pp. 76-153.

Granrud, Roman Constitutional History, Second Period, chapters vii-ix ; Third Period, chapters i-v.

1. Admission of the plebeians to the minor civil offices :
   (a) Curule aedileship.
   (b) Censorship, 351 B.C.

2. Publilian laws—Greater freedom of action for popular assemblies—Practical abrogation of *auctoritas patrum*, 339 B.C.

3. Praetorship opened to plebeians 337 B.C.

4. Priesthoods opened to plebeians by Ogulnian law, 300 B.C.

5. Hortensian law, 287 B.C.—Recognition of validity of resolutions (*plebis scita*) of Concilium Plebis.

6. General Character of the government in this period— The new nobility— An aristocracy of ex-officeholders— Supremacy of the Senate.

7. Reform of Comitia Centuriata—35 tribes—369 centuries (35 × 10 + 18 (*equites*) + 1 (*capite censi*).

8. Growing influence of the *Comitia Tributa*.

9. Beginnings of the provincial system.

10. Rise of the Equestrian Order—It becomes a capitalist class.

11. The clientship of this period.

LECTURE XXXIII.

CONSTITUTIONAL HISTORY OF REPUBLICAN ROME FROM THE AGE OF THE GRACCHI TO THE DEATH OF JULIUS CAESAR (133 TO 44 B.C.)—COLLAPSE OF THE REPUBLIC.

References.

How and Leigh, History of Rome, pp. 331-551.
Allen, Short History, pp. 147-220.
Granrud, Roman Constitutional History, Fourth Period.

1. Agrarian law of Tiberius Gracchus (133 B.C.)—Revolutionary measures employed for its adoption—Gracchus's murder—Execution of the law.

2. Gaius Gracchus (123 B.C.)—His reforms—Aims at at diminution of powers of nobility—His corn law—His death, 121 B.C.

3. The Conservative reaction after Gracchus's death.

4. Marius, Saturninus, Glaucia — Laws of Saturninus (100 B.C.).

5. The Social War—Drusus—The franchise granted to the Italians (90 B.C.).

6. The First Civil War—Laws of Sulpicius (88 B.C.)—Cinna, Marius, and Carbo—Triumph of Sulla (82 B.C.).

7. The Sullan constitution—Restoration of senatorial predominance—Sulla's death.

8. Conspiracy of Catiline (63 B.C.)—Significance of the movement.

9. First triumvirate (60 B.C.)—Caesar, Pompey, Crassus —Popular trend of affairs.

10. Conflict between Caesar and the Senate (49 B.C.).—Triumph of the monarchical idea—Caesar's rule (46–44 B.C.).

11. Review of the period—Forces at work—Causes of collapse of Republic.

LECTURE XXXIV.

THE ROMAN ASSEMBLIES.

References.

Ihne, History of Rome, vol. iv, pp. 9–41.
How and Leigh, History of Rome : see Index, under *comitia*.
Allen, Short History ; see Index, under Assemblies.
Ramsay, Manual, chapter iv.
Smith, Dictionary, under *comitia*.
Zöller, Römische Staatsaltertümer, p. 79 ff.
Gow, Companion to School Classics, p. 198 ff.
Granrud, Roman Constitutional History, Third Period, chapter iii.

A. Comitia Centuriata.

1. Method of convening *Com. Cent.*—The presiding officers : *consul* or *praetor—dies comitiales*.

2. Place of assembly—Outside *pomerium*.

3. Importance of the *auspicia—obnuntiatio—de caelo servare*—Other omens.

4. Methods of transacting business—In electing magistrates—In passing laws—In judicial cases.

5. Competency of *Com. Cent.*

B. Comitia Tributa and Concilium Plebis.

1. Origin and organization of *Com. Trib.*—outgrowth of *Concilium Plebis.*

2. The presiding magistrate—consul, praetor, curule aedile.

3. Place and time of meeting—The auspices.

4. Competency of the *Com. Trib.*
   (*a*) Elections.
   (*b*) Imposition of fines.
   (*c*) Laws introduced by consuls or praetors.

5. Competency of *Conc. Plebis.*
   (*a*) Election of plebeian magistrates.
   (*b*) Laws introduced by tribunes.
   (*c*) Judicial functions.

6. Conduct of business in *Com. Trib.*
   (*a*) Method of electing magistrates.
   (*b*) Procedure in judicial cases.
   (*c*) In legislation.

LECTURE XXXV.

ON MAGISTRACY IN GENERAL.

References.

Ihne, History of Rome, vol. iv, pp. 75–98.
Smith, Dictionary, under *magistratus.*
Zöller, Römische Staatsaltertümer, p. 135 ff.
Gow, Companion to School Classics, p. 182 ff.
Granrud, Roman Constitutional History, Second Period, chapter vi.

1. *Potestas, imperium*—General prerogatives inherent in all magistrates.

2. Classification of magistrates :
   (*a*) *Patricii* and *plebeii.*

(*b*) *Cum imperio* and *sine imperio*.
(*c*) *Majores* and *Minores*.
(*d*) *Curules* and *non-curules*.
(*e*) *Ordinarii* and *extraordinarii*.
3. Sequence of offices—Intervals between offices—Prescription as to age—Lex Villia Annalis.
4. Entrance upon office—Abdication and removal—Extension of terms.
5. Auspicia of magistrates.
6. Insignia and privileges.
7. Safeguards against abuse of power.
8. Table of historical development of Roman magistracy.

LECTURE XXXVI.

THE MAGISTRATUS MAJORES.

References.

Ihne, History of Rome, vol. iv, p. 117 ff.
Ramsay, Manual, p. 166 ff. ; 187 ff. ; 198 ff.
Smith, Dictionary, under *consul, praetor, censor*.
Zöller, Römische Staatstaltertümer, pp. 176–225.
Gow, Companion to School Classics, p. 173 ff.

A. The Consulship.

1. Meaning of the name *consul*—Earlier designations: *praetor, judex*.
2. Election and inauguration.
3. Military functions—Triumphs and ovations.
4. Civil functions—General executive—Initiative in legislation—Relations with Senate—Conduct of elections.
5. *Consulares—Proconsules*.

B. The Praetorship.

1. Origin and development.
2. Election—Insignia of office.

3. Functions.
  (*a*) Civil jurisdiction.
  (*b*) Conduct of *quaestiones perpetuae*.
  (*c*) Provincial administration.

C. The Censorship.

1. Origin and purpose of the office.
2. Term of service—Election—Inauguration.
3. Functions.
  (*a*) Taking of census.
  (*b*) *Recognitio equitum*.
  (*c*) *Lectio Senatus*.
  (*d*) *Regimen morum*.
  (*e*) Financial powers and duties.

LECTURE XXXVII.

THE MAGISTRATUS MINORES.

References.

Ihne, History of Rome, vol. iv, chapters vi, viii.
Ramsay, Manual, p. 194 ff., 189 ff., 175 ff.
Smith, Dictionary, under *quaestor, tribunus, aedilis*.
Zöller, Römische Staatsaltertümer, pp. 225–264.
Gow, Companion to School Classics, p. 177 ff.

A. The Quaestorship.

1. Origin—Name—Development of the office.
2. *Quaestores urbani*—Financial duties—Management of the *aerarium*.
3. Military quaestors—Management of war-chest—Become provincial servants.

B. The Tribunate.

1. Origin and development of the tribunate.
2. The Powers and Prerogatives of the tribunes:
  (*a*) Intercession: against magistrates, Senate, *comitia*.

(*b*) Positive functions—Legislative and judicial initiative in *Conc. Plebis*—Conduct of elections for tribunes and plebeian aediles.

(*c*) Prerogatives: *coercitio, jus cum plebe agendi, auspicia, edicta, jus senatum consulendi.*

4. Decay of tribunate.

C. Aedileship.

1. Origin and development of aedileship.
2. Duties of aediles.
   (*a*) *cura urbis.*
   (*b*) *cura annonae.*
   (*c*) *cura ludorum.*

LECTURE XXXVIII.

THE SENATE.

References.

Ihne, History of Rome, vol. iv, chapter ii.
Ramsay, Manual, p. 254.
Smith, Dictionary, under *Senatus.*
Zöller, Römische Staatsaltertümer, p. 287 ff.
Gow, Companion to School Classics, p. 191 ff.

1. Composition of the Senate—Patrician and plebeian elements—*Patres conscripti—curules—pedarii.*
2. Method of convening Senate—Time and places of meeting.
3. Procedure—Methods of voting.
4. Resolutions of the Senate :
   (*a*) *Senatus auctoritas.*
   (*b*) *Senatus consultum.*
   (*c*) *Senatus decretum.*
5. Competency of the Senate :
   (*a*) Participation in legislation.
   (*b*) In elections.

(*c*) Judicial functions.
(*d*) Religious control.
(*e*) Financial control.

6. Senate as director of foreign policy and diplomatic relations.

7. The Senate under the Empire.

LECTURE XXXIX.

ROMAN MILITARY ORGANIZATION.

References.

Ihne, History of Rome, vol. iv, chapter iv.
Judson, H. P., Caesar's Army.
Gow, Companion to School Classics, p. 221 ff.
Ramsay, Manual, p. 428 ff.
Zöller, Römische Staatsaltertümer, p. 348 f.

A. Army of the Republic.

1. Liability to service—Mode of levy.
2. The Legion—Strength—Organization—Officers.
3. Weapons and equipment.
4. Arrangement in battle—Tactics.
5. Marching order.
6. Methods of siege—Artillery.
7. Cavalry.
8. Auxiliaries.
9. The Roman camp.
10. Pay of soldiers—Discipline—Special rewards.

B. Changes in the Army.

1. Changes under Marius.
2. Changes under the Empire.
3. The city troops.
4. Auxilia.

LECTURE XL.

MONEY AND THE ROMAN FINANCIAL SYSTEM.

References.

Ihne, History of Rome, vol. iv, chapter vii.
Ramsay, Manual, p. 464 ff. ; p. 281 ff.
Gow, Companion to School Classics, p. 252 ff.
Zöller, Römische Staatsaltertümer, p. 318 ff.

1. Coinage—Metals used—Unit of reckoning—Different coins—Modern values—Notation.
2. The Roman revenues — *tributum* — *vectigalia* — From booty in war—*portoria*—Land revenues—Other sources.
3. Expenditures—Civil and military purposes—For public buildings—Religious purposes—For special donations.
4. Financial administration—Responsible officials—Methods of collecting revenues—Management of funds—The *fiscus* of the emperors.
5. Interest on money.

LECTURE XLI.

ROMAN JURISPRUDENCE.

References.

Gibbon, Decline and Fall of the Roman Empire, chapter xliv.
Hadley, Introduction to Roman Law, chapters, ii, iii.
Morey, Outlines of Roman Law.
Ramsay, Manual, p. 285 ff.
Gow, Companion to School Classics, p. 233 ff.
Zöller, Römische Staatsaltertümer, p. 379 ff.

1. Development of Roman law—Codes—Praetorian edicts —*Responsa*.
2. Private law :
   (*a*) Law of persons.
   (*b*) Law of property—Kinds of property—Titles— Transfers — Inheritance — The *centumviri—judices— arbitri—recuperatores*.

3. Lawyers—Emoluments.
4. Criminal law.
   (*a*) Crimes: political, civil.
   (*b*) Penalties.
   (*c*) Criminal process:—by people; by *quaestiones per-petuae;* by *assessores.*
   (*d*) Mode of procedure.
5. The Roman law as a contribution to civilization.
6. The Roman law as contrasted with Anglo-Saxon law.

LECTURE XLII.

ROMAN RELIGION AND WORSHIP.

References.

Mommsen, History of Rome, vol. i, book i, chapter xii ; book ii, chapter viii ; vol. iii, chapter xii ; vol. iv, chapter xii.
Ihne, History of Rome, vol. iv, chapter xiii.
Wilkins, Primer, p. 105.
Ramsay, Manual, p. 364 ff.
Tighe, Roman Constitution, p. 35 ff. ; p. 102 ff.
Madvig, Verfassung und Verwaltung des römischen Staates, vol. ii, p. 580 ff.
Granger, Frank, The Worship of the Romans.
Boissier, G., La Religion Romaine.
Allen, The Religion of the Ancient Romans, North American Review, vol. cxiii, pp. 30–62.
Clarke, J. F., Ten Great Religions, chapter viii.
Inge, Society in Rome, p. 1 ff.
Photographs : 98.030 ff.

1. The Roman religion as a system—Contrast with our modern conception of religion.
2. Original character of the Roman religion—Contrast with Greek religion.
3. Later de-nationalization and Hellenization of Roman religion.
4. The chief divinities.
5. The priestly colleges and their functions.
6. Worship—Sacrifices—Special cults.
7. Deification of the Emperors—The *Augustales.*

LECTURE XLIII.

ORGANIZATION AND ADMINISTRATION OF THE ROMAN DEPENDENCIES AND PROVINCES.

References.

Mommsen, The Provinces of the Roman Empire.
Ihne, History of Rome, vol. iv, chapter x.
Ramsày, Manual, p. 115 ff.; 218 ff.
Gow, Companion to School Classics, p. 209 ff.
Zöller, Römische Staatsaltertümer, p. 409 ff.

A. Italian Dependencies.

1. Different kinds of dependent Italian communities.
2. Colonies.
3. *Municipia*—Organization and government.
4. *Praefecturae*.
5. *Socii—Latini* and *Italici*—The *Lex Julia et Plautia Papiria*.
6. Augustus's division of Italy into regions.

B. The Provinces.

1. Administration of the Roman Provinces.
   (*a*) Under the Republic.
   (*b*) Under the Empire.
2. Civil and political status of the provincial communities and their citizens.